Booklets for Biblical Living

Letting Go of Legalism

Lou Priolo

Letting Go of Legalism

Kress Biblical Resources
The Woodlands, Texas
www.kressbiblical.com

ISBN: 978-1-934952-69-6

Cover Artwork: *The Harlowe Family, from Samuel Richardson's "Clarissa,"* by Joseph Highmore

Letting Go of Legalism

Several years ago, I was invited to speak at a rather large convention. Toward the end of the telephone conversation with the man who invited me, things took an unusual turn.

"Lou, I noticed by your photograph on the internet that you do not have any facial hair."

"I don't at the moment" I replied. "Actually, I just shaved off my winter beard."

"That's good because we have a policy that our speakers not have any facial hair as they are presenting."

"That shouldn't be a problem, but may I ask why?"

"Studies indicate that people don't trust people with facial hair."

After speaking with my fellow church elders, I politely declined the invitation. It was not just the facial hair requirement that led me (and the men) to say "no" to the offer, but also because it was commonly reported that the organization leaned towards promoting legalistic standards of behavior that led to critical, censorious attitudes among many of their attendees.

There is another, much more common, manifestation of legalism, one that I encounter as a Christian counselor quite regularly. It is when well-meaning parents develop a plethora of man-made rules for their children without being able to articulate the biblical basis for those rules. The legalism comes in when they 1) lead their children to believe that those rules are in essence God's rules, and 2) treat other parents who do not follow those rules as though they were inferior or bad parents. For example[1]:

- You mustn't let your toddler play with the remote control.
- You must place your infants on a strict feeding schedule according to Dr. So-and-So's scientifically based research (no exceptions).
- You must teach your infants sign language (because it is "not appropriate" for children to grunt or whine).
- If your child's so-called love language is "touch," you should never use corporal discipline.
- You should not allow your teenagers to go on dates.
- Cheerful "first-time obedience" is the only acceptable response to parental instruction.

Here are some other examples of legalism I have encountered over the years.

- Women should never wear pants.
- Singleness is a holier state than marriage.
- You shouldn't eat rabbit.[2]
- Dating is wrong; courting is biblical.
- It is wrong to practice any form of birth control.

---

1 Now for those of you who are parents, let me be clear: If you have adopted similar standards in your home, that is your prerogative. The legalism comes into play when you believe parents who do not insist on your standards for their households are somehow sinning, and thus you insist that other Christian parents adhere to the same standards. As I have explained elsewhere, it is also legalism if you do not explain to your children that these are your household rules (even though they may be based upon biblical principles) rather than God's directives. See *The Heart of Anger*.

2 The reason for this, as I remember, was based on the Old Testament dietary requirements and the fact that it supposedly required more calories to digest the rabbit than the rabbit, provided.

- You should not listen to anything but worshipful Christian or classical music.
- The best way to pray is by using a particular formula.
- Homeschooling is the only biblical way to educate children.

You may be reading this booklet because you have questions about the extent to which you struggle with legalism. So, before we go any further, here is a little inventory which will give you a general idea of the degree to which you might struggle with this issue. Using the grading scale below, evaluate yourself according to the frequency with which each statement is true of you:[3]

RATING SCALE	POINTS
Never (Hardly Ever)	5
Seldom	4
Sometimes	3
Frequently	2
Always (Almost Always)	1

1. When people hold differing opinions than I do about things that are not clearly delineated in Scripture, I judge them to be wrong, immature or unspiritual. _______
2. When I see other parents allowing their children to do things that I would not allow my children to do, even though no sin is involved, I judge them to be poor parents. _______
3. When other Christians disagree with me on minor doctrinal issues, I have difficulty fellowshipping with them. _______

3 The legalism behind some of these statements may not been readily apparent. Don't be too concerned if you cannot connect the dots between any individual question and your understanding of legalism at this point. Hopefully, by the time you have finished reading the book, the connection will become clearer.

4. When evaluating others, I err more on the side of judgment than I do on the side of mercy. ______
5. I focus more on correcting my external actions than on my internal attitudes. ______
6. My conscience is programmed more by the values, beliefs, scruples or approbation of my closest friends than it is by Bible. ______
7. I set high standards for myself (although I know that aren't necessarily in the Bible) and it bugs me that other Christians don't have the same convictions. ______
8. I beat myself up (am hard on myself for) for failures that I know don't displease God. ______
9. I believe all behavior is right or wrong, black or white; I don't leave much room for grey areas, or how God views the motivation behind that behavior. ______
10. I think God will love me more the more I obey Him. ______
11. I relate to God more as my Judge than as my loving Heavenly Father. ______
12. I am more concerned with the letter of the law than with the spirit of the law. ______
13. I tend to make decisions on the basis of my own internal list of do's and don'ts rather than on the basis of what would really please and honor God. ______
14. I am not consciously aware of my righteous standing before God (I don't have the assurance that all of my sins—past, present and future—have been covered by the blood of Christ). ______

15. I avoid certain Christians who don't agree with my personal standards of behavior (even thought I know those standards are not held by most believers). _______

16. To keep myself from disobeying God's laws, I add my own "mini-laws" and don't understand why others (or am critical of others who) don't do the same thing. _______

17. I rely more on my own righteousness (the fact that I try to obey God) than I do on His righteousness for my assurance that God is pleased with me. _______

18. I tell people what they should, must or ought to do in areas where the Bible is silent. _______

19. I find myself being more concerned about the doctrinal imperfections of people I know than I do my own sinful tendencies. _______

20. I am motivated to achieve certain things (to follow my self-imposed standards) more because I believe that doing so will make me look good to others, than that it will glorify God. (I do certain things more for the sake of my reputations than I do for the sake of God's reputation.) _______

There is a possible 100 point maximum. The lower the score, the greater is the likelihood of legalistic thinking. _______

What Legalism Is Not

Let's begin by taking a look at some common misperceptions or mistaken ideas about legalism. Christians can be very quick to falsely identify certain things as legalism and accuse others of being legalistic.[4]

4 This is especially true when they are on the receiving end of being reproved for their sin.

Legalism is not emphasizing obedience to God's Word. The church at which I ministered for sixteen years had a reputation to some in our community as being legalistic—largely because we placed a high priority on obedience to God's Word. But the Bible teaches us obedience from cover to cover. Jesus said:

> If you *love* Me, you will keep My commandments. (John 14:15, *emphasis added*)

In John 2:3–6 we read,

> And by this we know that we have come to know Him, *if we keep His commandments*. The one who says, "I have come to know Him," and does not keep His commandments, is a liar, and the truth is not in him; but whoever keeps His word, *in him the love of God has truly been perfected*. By this we know that we are in Him: the one who says he abides in Him ought himself to walk in the same manner as He walked. (*emphasis added*)

In John 15:10–11 Jesus says,

> If you *keep My commandments*, you will abide in My love; just as I have kept My Father's commandments, and abide in His love. These things I have spoken to you, that My joy may be in you, and that your joy may be made full. (*emphasis added*)

People who rightly interpret the Old and New Testament and seek to obey the clear directives and apply the clearly delineated principles of God's Word to their lives are not legalistic and should not be classified as such. Of course, there is some disagreement among evangelical Christians concerning the interpretation of certain passages. Care must be taken to show humility and tolerance towards those who hold to different views of these difficult passages.

Legalism is not necessarily the establishment of man-made rules. The Bible doesn't give us specific mandates for every area of life (principles and guidelines yes, but commands, no!). Man-made rules are sometimes needed in order for an organization, such as a family or a church, to function effectively.

We are commanded to pay taxes, obey our superiors, and submit to every ordinance (or institution) of man. Let's look at 1 Peter 2:13–14:

> Therefore submit yourselves to *every ordinance of man* for the Lord's sake, whether to the king as supreme, or to governors, as to those who are sent by him for the punishment of evildoers and for the praise of those who do good. (*emphasis added*)

When I was a student at Bible college, I had to sign a document agreeing to abide by certain man-made rules. There was a dress code, a hair code, a rule pertaining to the consumption of alcoholic beverages, and a dormitory curfew—all of which were man-made, extra-biblical regulations. But Calvary Bible College (now Calvary University) never even implied that these rules, in and of themselves, would make my life more pleasing to God. They simply explained that these were the school's rules, and as long as I chose to attend, I would have to obey them. Was that legalism? No.

Had they tried to convince me that these rules would make my life more pleasing to God, or that I would be obligated to obey them after I left college, that would have been legalism.

What Is Legalism?

You have probably experienced what you thought was legalism in your walk as a Christian. You may have been told by others that something you said was "legalistic." You doubtless, have on more than one occasion asked yourself, "Am I being legalistic about this matter?"

The construct of legalism is very broad. It encompasses many things—too many to adequately cover in a booklet of this size. Under the general heading there are subheadings. Legalism is a general category (or genus) under which there are subcategories (or subgenera).

GENRES OF LEGALISM

For the purpose of simplification, I have formulated a working definition of the kind of legalism this booklet was written to primarily address. ***Legalism is elevating man-made rules above the directives and principles that God has laid out in His Word;***[5] ***it is also judging others (accusing either in one's heart or with one's mouth) of sinning when those man-made rules are not followed.***[6]

According to James 4:11 which we will unpack in a few pages,[7] this form of legalism is sin. When we judge others for doing or not doing something as sin, which the Bible does not actually identify as sin, we are putting our standards above God's. We are judging God to have been negligent for not putting in the Bible what we think should have been put there.

Jesus said those who taught as doctrine the precepts of men, were hypocrites who were participating in vain worship (check out Matthew 15:9 and Mark 7:7). We will explore this definition and the James passage later in this booklet, but for now, let's get a clearer picture by looking at a few other descriptions of legalism.

John MacArthur provides us with a great general description of this kind of legalism:

> Legalism believes that every act, every habit, every type of behavior is either black or white. Legalists live by rules rather than by the Spirit. They classify everything as either good or bad, whether the Bible mentions it or not. They develop exhaustive lists of dos and don'ts. Doing the things on the

5 Or as RC Sproul would put it, legalism is "when we add legislation to God's law and treat the addition as if it were divine law." R. C. Sproul, *Before the Face of God: Book 1: A Daily Guide for Living from the Book of Romans*, electronic ed., (Grand Rapids: Baker Book House; Ligonier Ministries, 1992).

6 Another ironic tendency that legalists have in addition to falsely accusing others of sinning, is that they themselves sin overtly by gossip and slander. They make themselves look good as they "share" their overly censorious opinion of their brothers and sisters in Christ and impugn the good name of their victims through backbiting and insinuation.

7 You can take a peek at the passage now if you just can't wait.

> good list or avoiding the things on the bad list is their idea of spirituality, no matter what the inner person is like. Their lives are law controlled, not Spirit controlled. But refraining from doing things is not spiritually walking in the Spirit.[8]

Before we proceed with this genre of legalism, let's zoom out and take a brief look at some other forms of legalism.

Legalism is believing that salvation can be earned by obedience. The mindset is "justification is not obtained through *faith alone,* but rather by obedience to certain commandments."

Question 33 of the Westminster Shorter Catechism asks. "What is justification?" Here is the answer.

> Justification is an act of God's free grace, wherein he pardons all our sins, and accepts us as righteous in his sight, only for the righteousness of Christ imputed to us, and received by faith alone.

Note Romans 4: 5–8.

> But to the one who *does not work*, but believes in Him who justifies the ungodly, his faith is credited as righteousness, just as David also speaks of the blessing on the man to whom God credits righteousness apart from works: "BLESSED ARE THOSE WHOSE LAWLESS DEEDS HAVE BEEN FORGIVEN, AND WHOSE SINS HAVE BEEN COVERED. "BLESSED IS THE MAN WHOSE SIN THE LORD WILL NOT TAKE INTO ACCOUNT." (*emphasis added*)

As R.C. Sproul explains:

> The fundamental distortion of legalism is the belief that one can earn one's way into the kingdom of heaven. The Pharisees believed that due to their status as children of Abraham, and to

8 John F. MacArthur, Jr., *1 Corinthians* (Chicago: Moody Press, ©1984).

their scrupulous adherence to the law, they were the children of God. At the core, this was a denial of the gospel.[9]

Fundamentally, legalism is a motive that wants to establish (or otherwise improve) our standing before God by our own achievements. Legalism is the religion of human achievement. It argues that spirituality is based on Christ *plus* human works. It makes conformity to man-made rules the measure of spirituality.[10] The "works" part of the equation may take many forms, such as:

- Faith in Christ + obedience to the Law of Moses
- Faith in Christ + circumcision
- Faith in Christ + water baptism
- Faith in Christ + church membership
- Faith in Christ + adherence to every church doctrine of our church
- Faith in Christ + the proper diet
- Faith in Christ + appropriate Christian attire
- Faith in Christ + alignment with a particular political platform
- Faith in Christ + the proper approach to Christian parenting

We are saved by faith alone (faith + nothing)![11]

9 Sproul, R. C. (1996, c1992). *Essential Truths of the Christian faith*. Wheaton, Ill.: Tyndale House.

10 MacArthur, J. (1996, c1992). *Colossians* (Col 2:16). Chicago: Moody Press.

11 We are saved by faith alone but not the faith that is alone. In other words, it is not our works that save us in any way, but if we have saving faith based on Christ's righteousness having been imputed to us through our faith apart from our works (see Romans 3:21-31), our works will follow. They are the evidence that our faith is genuine. If we claim to have saving faith but have no works to substantiate that faith, we don't really have saving faith (see James 2:14-26).

Legalism is separating God's rules from the relationship He has established with us (the commands He has given from the covenant He has made with us). As R.C. Sproul would explain, legalism rips the commands out of their context. Our God is a god who has always given rules. God gave rules to Adam and Eve. He gave rules through Moses, through Christ, through some of the Apostles. But the rules were not given in abstraction. They were given in the context of a conventual relationship. The relationship came first, and the rules followed. To lose sight of the relationship, is to focus on the rules and to use them (obey them) for purposes other than for that which they were intended. They become rules for the sake of having rules.

To take the rules out of the relationship isn't a pretty thing. Think, for example, your favorite mountain range. Whatever or wherever it is, in the context in which God created it, it is beautiful. But how attractive would it be if someone took a truck load of that beautiful mountain range and dumped it smack dab in the middle of your living room?

With no relationship to set the rules into (out of which the rules flow), they serve no good purpose. Oh, to be sure, they might spare you from the misery associated with certain sin; they might add a few years to your life; they might give you a sense of accomplishment (like the false sense of righteousness that the self-deceived scribes and Pharisees had). But ultimately, they will frustrate you.

Legalism is ***believing that one can obey the Bible through one's own will and power for the purpose of gaining a greater measure of God's approval and favor***. Legalism is attempting to live the Christian life in one's own strength instead of relying on the supernatural grace God gives us through the Holy Spirit.

> Work out your salvation with fear and trembling; for it is God [the Holy Spirit] who is at work in you, both to will and to work for *His* good pleasure. (Philippians. 2:12-13, *emphasis added*)

The salvation we are commanded to work out in this passage is obviously not the destination of our soul after death. God has already worked that out for us through Christ's work on the cross. The directive to work out our salvation (or to bring it to completion) addresses our responsibility to actively participate in the work of progressive sanctification. So, to cooperate with the Spirit (and to let Him lead you), you must (by faith) do what the Bible says is necessary to grow as a Christian. But obedience to God's rules is the result of—not the means of—justification.

Regardless of the variety, legalism focuses on external rules rather than internal thoughts, attitudes, and motives. It concentrates on the letter of the law more than the spirit of the law. *Legalism is a manifestation of the sin of pride.* It thinks it knows better than God and that it is better than others.

There is another snare into which Christians sometimes step that may arguably be placed under this genre of legalism. It is more often referred to as ***moralism***. This form of legalism has to do with trying to follow the injunctions of Scripture without having the proper motivation for doing so (without understanding the realities of one's union with Christ). Some people live their whole lives sincerely trying to obey the commands of Scripture without having the proper motivation for doing so, because they haven't properly understood what has transpired when they were saved. In so doing, their attempts to do what the Bible says are often tainted with an "I've got to do this in order to earn more favor with God" mindset. Rather than having a "righteousness consciousness" (living all of their life in the full assurance that all of their sins—past, present and future—have been covered by the blood of Christ), they walk around carrying the burden of doing everything they can to ensure that God will somehow accept them.[12]

12 This is not the same thing as "making one's calling and election sure" (cf. 2 Peter 1:10). It is one thing, out of a heart of gratitude, to diligently strive to be godly, and, as a result, experience the assurance that your faith is genuine. It is quite another to believe that, by becoming a "godly person," your standing before God (or your favor in His eyes) changes for the better—that somehow, by your godliness, you have ingratiated yourself with Him.

When you became a Christian, you were placed in Christ[13]—you were baptized into His death, burial and resurrection. You now have a new identity—His identity. Where he went (to the cross, to the tomb, to the heavenly places), you went. Where He is, you are. You have been raised from the dead just as He was and are now positionally seated in heaven with Him. You are, in God's eyes (and hopefully in your own), righteous, because His righteousness has been imputed to you by virtue of your faith in Him. You now have an exalted status as an adopted son (a child of God), a co-heir with Christ, an ambassador for Christ.

All of this comes with tremendous privileges. And yes, this new position also comes with new responsibilities. But the responsibilities (the biblical injunctions) are to be done not in order to earn the new status, but out of a sense of gratitude for being given that new position. Throughout the New Testament, writer after writer in one way or another makes the point, "Here is your new heavenly position, so walk worthy of that new position."

Let's return to that form of legalism I am wanting to focus our attention upon throughout the remainder of this booklet. ***Legalism is elevating man-made rules above the directives and principles that God has laid out in His Word; it is judging others (accusing either in one's heart or with one's mouth) of sinning when those man-made rules are not followed.***

This is arguably the most toxic form of legalism. This is the legalism that elevates man-made rules (especially prohibitions) to the same level of authority as God-given commands. It is often accompanied with the belief that following these rules will aid one in his spiritual growth. This often extends to strict adherence to non-essential doctrinal positions as well as unconventional interpretations of certain

13 The phrase "in Christ" is by far the most common way the New Testament writers described those who are saved.

passages of Scripture. This brand of legalism is the one that those I counsel typically struggle with the most.[14]

Let's look at this matter of "higher standards" for a moment. The book of James addresses this issue quite succinctly. James writes:

> Do not speak against one another, brethren. He who speaks against a brother, or judges his brother, speaks against the law, and judges the law; but if you judge the law, you are not a doer of the law, but a judge of it. There is only one Lawgiver and Judge, the One who is able to save and to destroy; but who are you who judge your neighbor? James 4:11–12

How is it that by judging his brother the Christian judges the law? It's simple. By judging your brother to have done something wrong—something that the law (the Bible) does not specifically say is wrong (like requiring your infant to eat according to a particular schedule, or allowing your daughters to wear slacks or wear jewelry or use makeup, or eating pork or shrimp, eating at restaurants where the bar is front and center) you are also judging the Bible which neglected to mention the prohibition that you are convinced is so wrong. But this is not the worst of it!

Notice that the word *Lawgiver* (v.12, *NASV*) is in capital letters. This is because it is speaking of God. When you make extra-biblical judgments about your brother, you are making yourself a lawgiver and putting yourself in God's place. In fact, you are judging God! You are saying, in effect, "Everybody knows that it is wrong (or stupid or ridiculous) to do such a thing—why the Lord neglected to put that in Scripture, I can't imagine!" Can you see how arrogant that sentiment sounds? Do you see how proud it is to make such a judgment?

14 I am thinking especially of people who are "perfectionists." This would not only include a good number of people-pleasers, but also many with eating disorders, certain obsessions and compulsions, depressions, anxieties, fears and even indecisions and procrastinations. There is much more I want to say about perfectionism but that will have to wait for another booklet (God willing). But for now, simply consider that perfectionists, like legalists, raise the standard higher than the Scriptures. Legalists generally raise it higher for others; perfectionists raise it higher for themselves.

On a scale of one to ten (one being, "I regularly make very unloving, critical comments about others," and ten being, "I hardly ever make uncharitable judgments in my heart about others"), how critical are you of others? Before you answer, please read the following passages.

> Also do not take to heart everything people say, Lest you hear your servant cursing you. For *many times*, also, your own heart has known that *even you* have cursed others. (Ecclesiastes. 7:21–22, *emphasis added*)

> But *no one* can tame the tongue; it is a restless evil and full of deadly poison. With it we bless our Lord and Father, and with it we curse men, who have been made in the likeness of God; *from the same mouth come both blessing and cursing*. My brethren, these things ought not to be this way. (James 3:8-10, *emphasis added*)

The truth is, even though we know it is wrong, and even though we do not want others to do it to us, most of us make very unloving judgments about others regularly. Often the judgments of our heart gush out of our mouth.

> The mouth speaks out of that which fills the heart. The good man out of his good treasure brings forth what is good; and the evil man out of his evil treasure brings forth what is evil. (Matthew 12: 34b–35)

I like the way Richard Baxter sees it.

> Few people know the circumstances and reasons for what you do. They will presume to criticize you before they hear what you have to say. Had they done so, they would have absolved you of all charges in their own mind. It is rare to meet, even among professing believers who are sincerely committed [to

> Christ], those who are fearful and sensitive about sinning in this area of rash, ungrounded judging.[15]

It is sometime helpful to categorize this genre of legalism into two sections. There is the *doctrinal legalism* that has an elitist attitude toward those who don't cross every theological "t" and dot every theological "i" as precisely as they believe others should. And there is the *applied legalism* that requires of themselves and others comportment not required by Scripture.

WHAT ARE SOME CHARACTERISTICS AND MANIFESTATIONS OF LEGALISM?

If legalism is a sin (and I trust you are now beginning to see *why* it is a sin), and sin produces misery (and all sin does), then legalism will make you miserable! For various reasons, legalism robs you of joy and freedom. Have you ever been in a place, even temporarily, where your freedoms were restricted or taken away? If so, you know it wasn't fun. Allow me to connect the dots for you between the sin of legalism and sorrow. Put a check next to the box of any of the following items you know (or suspect) are true of you.

❒ ***Phariseeism*** (focusing on externals rather than internal matters of the heart). Legalism can turn you into a self-righteous Pharisee who uncharitably judges, criticizes, and condemns others. Jesus repeatedly used the word "woe" (Greek οὐαί) in reference to the Pharisees. In Matthew chapter 23 he pronounced eight woes upon them! We may rightly express the meaning of this word as "how greatly one will suffer" or "what terrible pain will come to one."[16] But not only does the heartache associated with this sin apply to the future, as with all sin, there will be temporal consequences as well. "Do not be deceived:

15 Baxter Richard, ***The Practical Works of Richard*** Baxter Vol.1, Soli Deo Gloria Publications, p. 188

16 Johannes P. Louw and Eugene Albert Nida, *Greek-English Lexicon of the New Testament based on Semantic Domains*, 1996, 1, 242.

God is not mocked, for whatever a man sows, that will he also reap" (Galatians 6:7; see also Proverbs 5:22, 14:14).

❒ ***Arrogance/Spiritual Blindness*** The root of legalism is almost always pride. And pride blinds us to our sin. Christian counselor Ed Welch explains.

> One of the most striking consequences of legalism is its invisibility to the legalist. Legalists tend to be blind to their own legalism. People will never come for counseling naming stubborn legalism as their problem. It always seems to be a problem for someone else or the church down the street. This is, in part, a result of legalism's tendency to follow laws of our own making.[17]

In Matthew 23 (the "Woe unto you" chapter mentioned above), Jesus repeatedly called the Pharisees blind. See for yourself and check out how many times he calls them blind.

> Woe to you, blind guides, who say, "If anyone swears by the temple, it is nothing, but if anyone swears by the gold of the temple, he is bound by his oath." You blind fools! For which is greater, the gold or the temple that has made the gold sacred? And you say, "If anyone swears by the altar, it is nothing, but if anyone swears by the gift that is on the altar, he is bound by his oath." You blind men! For which is greater, the gift or the altar that makes the gift sacred? So whoever swears by the altar swears by it and by everything on it. And whoever swears by the temple swears by it and by him who dwells in it. And whoever swears by heaven swears by the throne of God and by him who sits upon it.

17 Edward T. Welch, "Is Biblical-Nouthetic Counseling Legalistic? Reexamination of a Biblical Theme," *The Journal of Pastoral Practice* 11, no. 1 (1992): 12.

> Woe to you, scribes and Pharisees, hypocrites! For you tithe mint and dill and cumin, and have neglected the weightier matters of the law: justice and mercy and faithfulness. These you ought to have done, without neglecting the others. You blind guides, straining out a gnat and swallowing a camel!
>
> Woe to you, scribes and Pharisees, hypocrites! For you clean the outside of the cup and the plate, but inside they are full of greed and self-indulgence. You blind Pharisee! First clean the inside of the cup and the plate, that the outside also may be clean. (Matthew 23:16–26)

No less than five times does Jesus call these hypocritical, legalistic men blind! They focused their attention on the small stuff to such an extent that they neglected (couldn't even see with their peripheral vision) the important stuff. One of the greatest consequences of blindness to any sin (this one included) is the rejection one faces from others who see the pattern of sin in our lives and avoid us.

❒ ***Judgmental / Uncharitable Attitudes*** Viewing other Christians as second class is another snare (ancillary sin) into which legalists often fall.

> Critical persons are easily understood through the lens of legalism. Such persons are claiming that they have measured up to some legalistic standard. Their works-righteousness has put them in a position where they feel justified in judging others.[18]

Their works righteousness is a tricky thing. Many of them would probably cringe at the thought of earning one's salvation. But to the extent that they really believe in their hearts that (or even function as though) God is more pleased with them (or will show them more favor, or reward them more fully) due to their own self-imposed law

18 Edward T. Welch, "Is Biblical-Nouthetic Counseling Legalistic? Reexamination of a Biblical Theme," *The Journal of Pastoral Practice* 11, no. 1 (1992): 16.

(rules) and their desire to keep it (them), they are practicing a form of works-based righteousness.

Of course, they are often blinded to their own arrogance and how wicked their critical attitude really is in God's sight.[19] This may be because they have lost sight of the fact that their standard of judgment has become higher than the Bible's.[20] Or, it may be because they have lost sight of their own sinfulness. As a result of straining out gnats, they have swallowed camels (vs. 24).

I remember as young man being very influenced by a famous Bible teacher. God used this man's teaching to radically change my life in many good ways. I am thankful for his influence. But in the process of learning all I could from him, I imbibed much of his legalism. The most obnoxious (and probably the more sinful) part of it was not the man-made rules (disguised as "God's higher standards") I followed, but a very subtle, holier than thou attitude towards other Christians who were either ignorant of, or unwilling to follow, some of his teachings.[21] It wasn't until God sent into my life someone who was more of a follower of this man than I was that I saw how repugnant this arrogant attitude was. I remember praying, "Lord, if this is the way I am representing myself to others, I repent from the depths of my soul." It was seeing this fellow-follower's air of superiority (the way he viewed himself as a "special Christian" and the way he subtly looked down on others) that brought me to repentance. I pray the Lord has since opened his eyes.

---

19 It may also be that in their evaluation of others, they favor *judgment* over *mercy* rather than vice versa. If we must err between the two, we are to err on the side of mercy. "Mercy triumphs over judgment" (James 2:13; see also Matthew 9:9-13).

20 Some legalists know very well that their self-imposed standards are higher than God's, but believe He is nonetheless *more* pleased with their willingness to do even *more* than He requires—that He is *more* pleased with them than He is with those who don't follow their standards (or who don't try to go above and beyond). Some have been taught these "higher standards" by other legalists, never realizing that they were imbibing legalistic doctrine (in some cases doctrines of demons).

21 This self-righteous attitude also morphed into a kind of doctrinal self-righteousness (you might even call it "doctrinal legalism") that was not only somewhat intolerant of those who had minor doctrinal differences with me, but saw them as semi-heretics, and therefore, not as pleasing to God as I, because I was such a careful theological student.

❐ ***Ungraciousness (If Not Unforgiveness)*** Since most forms of legalism are rooted in not understanding the grace of God, legalists often struggle with being gracious to others. Not only do they raise the standard of behavior above the scriptural level, they may also inordinately want (if not demand) those who violate the standards (God's and theirs) to be held accountable for their "transgressions," overlooking the forgiveness and restoration they are biblically required to grant and the mercy and kindness they are required to show to sinners (especially repentant sinners).

❐ ***Hypocrisy*** I have observed among legalistic individuals I have known a tendency to strain out theological gnats while they swallow hamartiological camels.[22] For the sake of doctrinal integrity, they will argue tooth and nail for an abstruse point of theology yet judge, censure, disrespect, and gossip about others whose theology is not quite as pristine as theirs. They are intolerant. They slander and backbite about, are rude and unkind toward, and even belittle those not in their theological clique. Some of them even have misogynistic attitudes. Woe unto them! May the Lord help them to see and repent of their sin before they hurt anyone else.

❐ ***Disassociation with True Believers*** Legalism can cause unnecessary divisions among Christians. What is even worse than this judgmental attitude is refusing to associate with (to separate oneself from) Christians who don't hold to the same legalistic "higher standards" as they do. "I will only associate with (or have as my close friends) people who agree with my understanding of what it really means to please God." In Proverbs chapter 6:16-19, Solomon identifies things that the Lord hates. The last one is what he hates the most.

> *There are six things that the Lord hates, seven that are an abomination to him: haughty eyes, a lying tongue, and hands that shed innocent blood, a heart that devises wicked plans, feet that make*

---

22 Hamartiology is the doctrine of sin. It is taken from the Greek word ἁμαρτία (hamartia), to err or miss the mark.

> *haste to run to evil, a false witness who breathes out lies, and one who sows discord among brothers.*" (Proverbs 6:16–19, ESV)

Do you really want to be responsible for doing this?

Richard Baxter addressed separation caused by a censorious attitude many years ago.

> Censoriousness causes unkindness and sinful separation in the censurers; when they have falsely thought their brothers to be worse than they are, they must then reproach them or have no communion with them, and avoid them as too bad for the company of people such as themselves.[23]

This censorious (critical and disapproving) attitude, which is sinful in and of itself, is made worse because it is based upon fallacious, man-made distortions of what is necessary to please God. I know of professing Christians in the same family who will not associate with other family members because of so called "sins" that have little to no biblical basis.[24] Legalism is contagious. It is leaven, and a little leaven leavens the whole lump. Beware of infecting others with your disease.

❒ ***Fear of Failure*** The fear of failure is not only a byproduct of the sin of legalism, but it is also something that feeds (is a catalyst for developing more) legalism.

> No other theme in Scripture describes the experience of fear of failure as well as legalism. Fear of failure points to a concern for our performance and reputation. It betrays a theology that says, "I must measure up so I can find personal meaning in myself. Also, I must measure up so others will think I am successful."[25]

23 Baxter, Volume 1 p.864 paraphrased.

24 This seems to occur most often with in-law relationships.

25 Edward T. Welch, "Is Biblical-Nouthetic Counseling Legalistic? Reexamination of a Biblical Theme," *The Journal of Pastoral Practice* 11, no. 1 (1992): 15.

It is not primarily the fear of failing God (sinning) that is in view here, but rather the fear of not succeeding in what one has set out to accomplish. If I fail to do what God requires, I know my sins are covered, because I am in Christ. But Christ did not promise to cover the feelings of inadequacy that are the result of my failing to live up to my own unbiblical standards.[26] It is not necessarily a sin to fail to accomplish everything one sets out to do. The Apostle Paul made plans to minister to people in places he apparently never was able to visit. The fear of failure didn't keep him from planning or even from announcing his plans (intentions) to others.

But legalistic people who are afraid of failing in areas where it is not a sin to fail, tend to feed their legalistic mindset by reinforcing whatever manmade "don'ts" will prevent potential failure or minimize damage to their success-to-failure ratio (batting average of accomplishments).

❒ ***Perfectionism*** Legalistic Christians frequently find themselves struggling with perfectionism. In fact, I view (and treat) "perfectionism" as legalism on steroids. Not only do perfectionists fear failure, they typically fear anything less than flawlessness. To them, getting a B+ (or sometimes even an A-) is as bad as getting an F.[27] And for perfectionists, this unrealistic expectation of getting straight A's is not limited to schoolwork, but extends to every area of life. In every responsibility they have been given (or take upon themselves), they must excel to the max. The aim of every endeavor is not, as the Bible requires, to be "faithful," but rather to be exceptional and extraordinary (if not incomparable to all competitors). Imperfection is intolerable—a fate almost worse than death!

❒ ***Anger (Frustration with Self and Others)*** Because their expectations of themselves and of those with whom they have to interact are unrealistically high (and therefore frequently unachievable), they

26 For more about this topic, see my booklet entitled, *Self-Image: Overcoming Inferiority Judgments*, Presbyterian and Reformed Publishing.

27 I know of cases where perfectionistic people judged themselves to be failures even after getting an A+ because they reasoned, "I had to work harder than others who got an A+, so I am not as perfect as they are."

become easily frustrated (provoked to anger as a result of failure to perform). This anger may manifest itself in a variety of ways; most notably by an impatient, irritable, demanding, and critical spirit.

❒ ***Frequent Conflicts and Quarrels (Strained Relationships)*** The legalist's self-righteous and judgmental spirit (not to mention the fact that he is perceived to be a party-pooper) causes others to push back against him. His rigid, myopic (or unsystematic),[28] no-exceptions, letter-of-the-law interpretation and application of certain Scripture passages tempt others to flee from him. His unwillingness to consider other perspectives about things that are not clearly delineated in the Bible causes others to see him as unreasonable—and rightly so. He often stubbornly holds to his views, refusing to acknowledge that there are presently, and have been throughout history, other orthodox Christians who see things differently. He does not consider that "mercy triumphs over judgment" (James 2:13).

❒ ***Inordinate People-Pleasing*** The legalist is often motivated by a desire to "look good" (or to be more spiritual) in the eyes of others, and consequently looks more to correcting outward behavior than issues of the heart. If you struggle with legalism, you may also be a people-pleaser who, at some level, loves the approval of man more than the approval of God.[29] As J. I Packer explains,

> A good deed is one done (1) according to the right standard (God's revealed will, i.e., his moral law), (2) from a right motive (the love to God and others that marks the regenerate heart), and (3) with a right purpose (pleasing and glorifying God, honoring Christ, advancing his kingdom, and benefiting one's neighbor).

28 By "unsystematic" I am speaking in terms of systematic theology which looks at everything the Scriptures have to say about a topic rather than one or two verses.

29 I have written more extensively about this subject in ***Pleasing People: How to Not Be an "Approval Junkie,"*** Presbyterian and Reformed Publishing.

> Legalism is a distortion of obedience that can never produce truly good works. Its first fault is that it skews motive and purpose, seeing good deeds as essentially ways to earn more of God's favor than one has at the moment. Its second fault is arrogance. Belief that one's labor earns God's favor begets contempt for those who do not labor in the same way. Its third fault is lovelessness in that its self-advancing purpose squeezes ***humble kindness*** and ***creative compassion*** out of the heart.[30]

❒ ***Over-Identification with Vocation or Ministry*** There is a tendency for perfectionistic Christians (who again are typically legalistic ones) to put more time, effort, and thought into their job or ministry than they should. What I mean by that is a tendency to have misplaced priorities: They strive hard to get straight A's (good reviews) at work, but neglect (are willing to fail in) their other God-given responsibilities (like ministering to their spouse and children). What is worse, they can grow to see and identify themselves (categorize themselves) as being more valuable as a worker of their calling or "craft" than as a Christian, a spouse, a parent, a church member, a friend, etc.

❒ ***Spiritual Damage to One's Children*** It pains me tremendously to even have to add this one to the list. I know of countless brokenhearted parents whose children have either turned away from the faith completely or whose faith has been otherwise damaged, in part because of legalism and its attending sins. Religion to these children at some point became unappealing and unreasonable because it was little more than a set of unreasonable rules (or tedious doctrines). Parents must have a set of man-made "rules of the house" in order to keep order in a family of sinners. But to not teach children the difference between temporary man-made rules which they will only be required to obey so long as they are a part of the household, from God's rules, which they will always be obligated to obey, is to set them up for failure.

30 Packer, J. I., ***Concise Theology*** Wheaton, Ill.: Crossway, 2020, p. 189-190. Emphasis added.

Indeed, it may even be to teach them a false gospel. Legalism is a communicable disease![31]

THE SINFULNESS OF LEGALISM

Although most Christians would agree that legalism is problematic in many ways, few seem to fully come to grips with the reality that legalism is a sin. Think for a moment about our Lord's anger. He was sinless; therefore, all of his anger was righteous. What is it that provoked Him to anger more frequently than anything else? Was it not the legalism and hypocrisy of the religious leaders of His day? Jesus' anger at them proves the sinfulness of legalism.

Let's take a look at another biblical woe associated with legalism. Check out the first line of this notable quote from the book of Isaiah (5:20, ESV, *emphasis added*):

> *Woe to those who call* evil good
>   and *good evil,*
> who put darkness for light
>   and light for darkness,
> who put bitter for sweet
>   and sweet for bitter!

To call something evil that God has called good (something that He has not specifically or broadly classified as sin)—something that He has created for his people to enjoy and in so doing glorify Him though thanksgiving—is a serious thing!

> Now the Spirit expressly says that in later times some will depart from the faith by devoting themselves to deceitful spirits and teachings of demons, through the insincerity of liars whose consciences are seared, who forbid marriage and require

31 It is transmitted not only from parents to children, but also from friend to friend and from shepherds to their flocks.

> abstinence from *foods that God created to be received with thanksgiving by those who believe and know the truth. For everything created by God is good, and nothing is to be rejected if it is received with thanksgiving, for it is made holy by the word of God and prayer.* (1 Timothy 4:1–5, ESV, *emphasis added*)

> Behold, what I have seen to be good and fitting is to eat and drink and *find enjoyment* in all the toil with which one toils under the sun the few days of his life that God has given him, for this is his lot. Everyone also to whom God has given wealth and possessions and *power to enjoy them*, and to accept his lot and *rejoice* in his toil—*this is the gift of God.* (Ecclesiastes 5:18–19, ESV, *emphasis added*)

> God… richly provides us with everything to enjoy. (1 Timothy 6:17)

> The one who observes the day, *observes it in honor of the Lord.* The one who eats, *eats in honor of the Lord, since he gives thanks to God*, while the one who abstains, abstains in honor of the Lord and *gives thanks to God.* (Romans 14:6, ESV, *emphasis added*)

> "If *I partake with thankfulness*, why am I denounced because of that for which I give thanks? So, whether you eat or drink, or whatever you do, *do all to the glory of God.*" (1 Corinthians 10:30–31, ESV, *emphasis added*)

When we, through legalism, bind the consciences of other believers with man-made prohibitions that are above and beyond what the Bible clearly prescribes for sons and daughters to glorify God and enjoy Him, we put a stumbling block in their paths in several ways. Not only do we prevent them from thanking God for His provision, robbing God of a portion of His glory, but we make these "new" commandments a burden to our brothers that He never intended them to carry. His yoke is supposed to be easy and His burden light. Instead, like the religious leaders of His day we "tie up heavy burdens and lay them on men's shoulders" (Matthew 23:4).

> When you study the life of Christ, it is noteworthy how He deliberately did things to provoke the legalists. He could have healed people on any other day of the week, but He often did it on the Sabbath. He could have been more discreet in violating the Pharisees' rules, but He did it openly. When a Pharisee invited Jesus to dinner, He could have gone along with their elaborate hand-washing custom, but He deliberately ignored it. When they questioned Him about it, He could have been more polite, but He blasted them for their hypocrisy. When a lawyer pointed out that Jesus had offended them as well, He didn't say, "I'm sorry! I didn't mean to offend you good folks." He said, "Woe to you lawyers as well!" Jesus confronted legalism as sin.[32]

Legalism is a sin because it is rooted in pride. It is a sin because it effectively adds things to God's Word that He didn't include in His Book (but presumably should have). It is a sin because it focuses on external things while ignoring matters of the heart. It is a sin because (or at least when) it causes you to uncharitably judge your brother in Christ who doesn't hold to your high and extrabiblical standard. It is a sin because it is contrary to grace. Although the term legalism is not found in the Bible, the establishing of extra-biblical rules for the purpose of aiding in one's sanctification is denounced.

> If with Christ you died to the elemental spirits of the world, why, as if you were still alive in the world, do you submit to regulations—"Do not handle, Do not taste, Do not touch" (referring to things that all perish as they are used)—according to human precepts and teachings? These have indeed

32 Stephen Cole, https://bible.org/seriespage/lesson-57-why-jesus-hates-legalism-luke-1137-54

> an appearance of wisdom in promoting self-made religion and asceticism and severity to the body, but they are of no value in stopping the indulgence of the flesh. (Colossians 2:20–23, ESV)

No value! Think about that. Adding regulations based upon man's precepts and teachings to what the Bible says is necessary is something Scripture warns Christians against doing.

"THAT'S NOT APPROPRIATE"

There is a phrase that legalists often use that I would like to briefly address, although in many contexts it is a perfectly good and fitting expression. The phrase I'm referring to is, "it's not appropriate." It can be subtly used to inflict guilt upon its intended targets. Now there is nothing wrong with trying to help people see their sin (indeed, it is right and necessary to do so). But if the Scriptures have been given for this express purpose (See 2 Timothy 3:16-17), why not use *them*? If something is not appropriate, and its inappropriateness is not clearly evident, shouldn't an explanation follow that clarifies the biblical basis for using the term? Wouldn't it be better, in many cases, to simply make the argument directly from the Scripture? If no supporting Scripture can be found, perhaps the phrase shouldn't be used in that particular context.

AM I A LEGALIST?

Based on what you have read so far, please record on the spaces below the specific rules or rubrics that you follow, which you believe or suspect cannot be substantiated with a clear biblical directive or solid biblical principle. Also, record the behaviors and activities you believe you have uncharitably judged other for doing (or not doing). As you read the next section of the booklet, come back and see if you can apply what follows to adjust your thinking (repent of) about these matters.

My Legalist Tendencies	What I Can Do to Change

Letting Go of Legalism

What can be done to counteract the legalistic tendencies you have identified thus far in reading this booklet? More than you may have realized. Listed below are a few biblically-based suggestions you may want to consider as you move to a more grace-oriented way of thinking.

Make it your goal to thoroughly appreciate and appropriate the doctrine of justification (and while you are at it, your union with Christ). There is a lot to learn, appreciate and apply in these two doctrines. We all should strive to comprehend them more than we did at first (when we first understood the Gospel). But legalistic individuals (people with over-scrupulous consciences) and perfectionistic individuals (those with an "all-or-nothing" standard of performance) will benefit tremendously from diving deep into these truths and drinking freely of them.

If you are in any way following legalistic rules because you believe that by doing so you will be earning extra brownie points with God, or that somehow he will love you more because of your strict adherence to your self-imposed, man-made rules, you have missed the mark. You may even, to some extent, have fallen from (or never really understood) grace (see Galatians 5:1-6). You will especially be helped by marinating your mind in these truths.

One particular aspect of our union with Christ that many with legalistic tendencies find especially helpful is that of *adoption*. Through Christ (and our being united to Him) we have all become sons and daughters of God. Before we were in Christ we related to the Divine Being as our Judge. Now, we relate to him as our Heavenly Father, indeed Abba Father (Papa, Daddy; see Romans 8:15; Galatians 4:4-7).[33] The legalist may struggle to see God as his loving and merciful[34] Heavenly Father because he focuses so much on rules (law) and so little on grace and mercy. It will be easier for him to let go of his superfluous rules by focusing more on his relationship as a son. In fact, he might not be able to let go of the one without embracing the other.

There is a reason why most of the New Testament epistles begin with what some have referred to as "positional truth." The authors typically didn't begin by giving injunctions (rules if you please), but by reminding the saints of their new position before God in Christ. Perhaps the reason for this is that they wanted their readers to understand that the injunctions that come towards the end of the books are to flow out of one's understanding of what Christ has done for them (what it means to be *in Christ*), at the beginning of the books. Perhaps they realized that to begin with rules, would tempt many (remember the human heart is a legalistic one) to obey the rules out of a sense of mere duty more than out of a sense of gratitude and love for Christ. (Jesus said, "if you *love* me, you will *keep* my commandments (*obey* my rules.")[35] Perhaps they knew that without unpacking the doctrine of justification and union with Christ first, people might be tempted to think that their obedience was a means of acquiring more of God's favor or love or acceptance.

Here are some recommendations to help you marinate your mind in positional truth.

33 Our Heavenly Father may very well discipline us when we sin, but such discipline is motivated by love. It is redemptive rather than retributive.

34 "Be merciful, just *as your Father is merciful*." (Luke 6:36, NASB95, emphasis added)

35 It's Christ's rules (not our rules) that we are to obey.

- Read and reread those books of the Bible that emphasize justification by grace through faith and your union with Christ (for example, Romans, Ephesians and Galatians), asking God to help you understand the initial portions of those books that speak of your position and standing before your Heavenly Father.
- Memorize and meditate upon specific verses that help you understand grace.
- Learn how to use trusted commentaries to help you understand what you are reading.
- Ask your spiritual shepherds to recommend books (and podcasts) that make these things plain.[36]

Learn to distinguish sin issues from non-sin issues. God doesn't want his children to remain infants who can only drink milk. He wants all of us to be mature (to grow up) and to sustain ourselves with solid food. He wants us to know the difference between what is right and what is wrong.

> But solid food is for the mature, who because of practice have their senses trained to discern good and evil. (Hebrews 5:14)

> *Woe to those who call* evil good, and *good evil.* (Isaiah 5:20a, *emphasis added*)

If we do not know the difference between what is a really a sin and what is not actually a sin (what is good and what is evil), it is an indication that we are not as mature as we should be. We are told to train our faculties[37] according to the Word of God.

---

36 I especially like the book *Perfect Sinners* by Matt Fuller.

37 The word for "senses" here is ***aisthētēria*** (GK: αἰσθητήρια), having to do with our capacity to perceive something. Our conscience is the primary place where this particular capacity of distinguishing between good and evil resides.

The Bible makes a distinction between those who are weak in faith (weaker brothers—those whose faith to partake of certain things is underdeveloped)—and those who are strong (stronger brothers; those who have the faith that they can partake of all kinds of things).

> As for the one who is weak in faith, welcome him, but not to quarrel over opinions. One person believes he may eat anything, while the weak person eats only vegetables. Let not the one who eats despise the one who abstains, and let not the one who abstains pass judgment on the one who eats, for God has welcomed him. Who are you to pass judgment on the servant of another? It is before his own master that he stands or falls. And he will be upheld, for the Lord is able to make him stand. (Romans 14:1–4, ESV)

The warning given to the stronger brother is to not despise or hold in contempt (or belittle) the weaker brother. The warning to the weaker is not to judge the stronger. The legalist may perceive himself as the stronger, more mature Christian, but to the degree that his conscience is plagued with scruples that are not solidly supported by Scripture, he may very well be the weaker Christian.

Perhaps it would be helpful to think of your conscience as a computer, and legalism as a virus that needs to be eradicated from your hard drive. Or maybe the better correlation would be the conscience being analogous to a small electronic device (like a cellphone or WiFi router) that needs a firmware upgrade. If you are a Christian, your conscience is reprogrammable. You must connect your device directly to (plug it into) the download source which is the Word of God. But first you must make sure all alien programs are shut down (if not totally uninstalled from the device). By this I mean that you must recognize and, if possible, remove from your life those things that influence your thinking away from the truth of Scripture.[38]

Don't fall into the trap of those who opposed Jesus. What was their error? Christ often contended with the religious leaders of His day over this particular genre of legalism. The scribes and the Pharisees held to and elevated the oral tradition (the Talmud) to such an extent that it became as legal and binding to some of them as the Scriptures, if not more so. It was to these leaders, who did not distinguish man-made from God-breathed commandments, that Christ, after calling them hypocrites, reiterated the words of Isaiah 29:13, "This people honors me with their lips, but their heart is far from me. But in vain do they worship me, teaching as doctrines the precepts of men" (Matthew 15:8–9).

Make sure the rules you are living by are in fact biblical—that they are indeed God's rules. And if they are not clear directives of Scripture, but rather based on solid biblical principles (that is, if they are "biblically-derived" rules), you must take care that you do not turn them into universal laws, either for yourselves or for others. Ask yourself, do these rules really apply to every other Christian in every other culture around the world? If not, be very careful about their application.

Don't allow your own fear of falling into sin skew your thinking about the sinfulness of certain activities. As I look back over some of my former legalistic tendencies, I must admit that some of them came out of a healthy fear of falling into certain sins. After all, Proverbs 22:3 gives us this caution, "The prudent sees danger and hides himself, but the simple go on and suffer for it."

Sometimes, however, our fear of danger can become inordinate and cause us to find extreme ways to avoid temptation. We become secure in the belief that these measures have helped us not fall into sin. Since they work for us, we recommend them to (if not impose them on) others. Even when our fear of falling is reasonable, we must take care not to force our self-imposed, rightly-motivated, extra-biblical restrictions on

38 For example, since the conscience of a people pleaser, has, to some extent, been "programmed" to please people (to follow the rules of certain people) more than God, it will have to be reprogrammed by the Scriptures to think first about what will please God.

others. Not everyone needs to follow the exact same protocol for handling temptation.[39] There is often more than one way to biblically skin a catfish. It might be right or even best for *you* to flee or to avoid temptation by restricting *yourself* from certain non-sinful activities or events, but "to his own master" your brother will stand or fall.

> Who are you to pass judgment on the servant of another? It is before his own master that he stands or falls. And he will be upheld, for the Lord is able to make him stand. (Romans 14:4)

We also must be careful that we do not allow our fear of sinning to lead us to exercise inordinate (extra-biblical) control over those under our spiritual care by going beyond what the Scriptures require. Imposing unbiblical requirements on our subordinates because we don't trust God as we should is an abuse of our authority. It is also laying a dangerous snare before them.

Don't major on minor issues. This is what the legalists of Jesus' day did.

> Woe to you, scribes and Pharisees, hypocrites! For you tithe mint and dill and cumin, and have neglected the weightier matters of the law: justice and mercy and faithfulness. These you ought to have done, without neglecting the others. You blind guides, straining out a gnat and swallowing a camel! (Matthew 23:23–24, ESV)

R. C. Sproul explains how this kind of legalism can lead to imbalanced living (if not hypocrisy).

39 This is something I, as a biblical counselor, strive be mindful of when I am advising others: If God doesn't require one of His children to do something, neither should I. So, the advice I give that is based more upon biblical principles than on clear directives, is more along the lines of, "Unless you have a better idea, perhaps you should consider doing this."

> Another form of legalism is majoring on the minors. Jesus rebuked the Pharisees for omitting the weightier matters of the law while they were scrupulous in obeying minor points (Matthew 23:23-24). This tendency remains a constant threat to the church. We have a tendency to exalt to the supreme level of godliness whatever virtues we possess and downplay our vices as insignificant points. For example, I may view refraining from dancing as a great spiritual strength while considering my covetousness a minor matter.[40]

This is especially important in the area of doctrine. In the final analysis, yes, even small doctrinal error is sin. Moreover, because the truth is not plural, and "no prophecy of Scripture is of any private interpretation",[41] if two people hold differing positions on the same interpretation of a particular passage (or doctrine), *at least* one of them is wrong. But many things about which orthodox Christians disagree we may not be certain of until the Lord returns. So, there is a place for us to be forbearing with brothers and sisters of "like precious faith" who hold to positions on minor doctrinal matters that differ from ours.

Shift your focus from the external to the internal. "The Lord sees not as man sees: man looks on the outward appearance, but the Lord looks on the heart." If the Sermon on the Mount teaches anything, it teaches that God is more concerned with attitudes of the heart than he is with external behavior. As a counselor, I am often asked, "Is it a sin for me to . . .?" My response often is, "Tell me your motive for doing it, and I'll tell you whether or not it is a sin." Drinking alcohol, smoking a recreational cigar, wearing an article of clothing, going to a particular movie, or to a party where unbelievers will likely be sinning are not in and of themselves forbidden in Scripture. The thing that God cares about is *why* you want to partake. Can you do so for the

40 Sproul, R. C. (1996, c1992), *Essential truths of the Christian faith*. Wheaton, Ill.: Tyndale House.

41 2 Peter 1:20

glory of God and for the eternal benefit of your neighbor? That is the thing that matters most.

So often we think that what makes something a sin is the questionable activity itself, but God is concerned about our motives for participating in the activity more than He is about the activity itself. Jesus said, "Do not judge according to appearance, but judge with righteous judgment" (John 7:24 NKJV). The legalist will condemn activities as sinful without regard for the motive of the person doing or participating in the activity. The person who judges with "righteous judgment" will get below the surface of the activity itself and not pronounce judgment prematurely. And if he cannot do so (if he is not in a position to ask about motives), he will withhold judgement and try to presume the best about the person's motives. (Love believes all things—it believes the best; 1 Corinthians 13:7).

Exercise great care in judging others, because you will be judged by the same standard you use for them.

> Do not judge, so that you will not be judged. For in the way you judge, you will be judged; and by your standard of measure, it will be measured to you. Why do you look at the speck that is in your brother's eye, but do not notice the log that is in your own eye? Or how can you say to your brother, "Let me take the speck out of your eye," and look, the log is in your own eye? You hypocrite, first take the log out of your own eye, and then you will see clearly to take the speck out of your brother's eye! (Matthew 7:1-5)

Do you know what Jonathan Edwards, Charles Spurgeon, G. Campbell Morgan, Martyn Lloyd-Jones, and C. S. Lewis all had in common? They all smoked. Of course, they also all lived before the dangers of smoking were fully realized. But the fact is that God used them mightily despite the fact that they were smokers.

What kind of filter do you use to determine whether the judgments you make about others are biblical? Here are a few questions you might want to ask yourself as you are evaluating the activities and behavior of others.

- Am I uncharitably judging the motives of the person who is participating in this activity/behavior?
- Am I uncharitably judging the spirituality of the person who is participating in this activity/behavior?
- Am I imposing my personal preferences on the person who is participating in this activity/behavior?
- Does the Bible expressly forbid this activity/behavior? Or, even though there may be biblical principles that might discourage *me* doing it myself, is there nothing in the Bible prohibiting it?
- Is there any way that this activity may be done to the glory of God? (Am I certain that there is no way the person I am about to judge, can do what he is doing to the glory of God?)
- Do I have some kind of a sinful attitude (bitterness, jealousy, envy) toward the person participating in this activity that might be affecting (skewing) my judgment?
- Could it be that in this matter I am a weaker brother and the person participating in this behavior is the stronger brother?

Let me ask you one concluding question: "Why do we as Christians try to keep God's commandments?"[42]

A few years ago, I came across these thoughts in an on-line sermon. I don't think I can improve upon them:

We do not keep God's commands in order to improve our standing with God. We do not keep God's laws [try to do what the Bible commands] in order to win His love, or to get more of His love. Rather,

- We keep God's commands as an expression of our <u>love</u> for Him.

42 Asking your legalistic counselee to answer this question as a homework assignment (and going over its answer in session) might be quite beneficial.

- ❒ We keep God's commands as a show of our loyalty to Him.
- ❒ We keep God's laws as an act of devotion to Him.
- ❒ We keep God's laws out of gratitude to Him.[43]

And we do not—we dare not—add to God's laws and unlawfully impose our man-made rules, regulations and preferences upon others.

I would like to leave you with a final citation from Ed Welch's fine article.

> The truth is that legalism is a plague that affects us all. Each of us has some remaining tendency to "want to be under the law" (Galatians 4:21). Legalism is a "temptation that is common to man" (1 Corinthians 10:13). It is not extinguished at conversion. Although we are sinners who are forgiven and empowered to fight against sin, our sin continues to exert itself. One persistent form of sin is to look for some foundational righteousness in ourselves, even if it is only a little righteousness.[44]

John Calvin said the human heart is a factory (forge) of idols. By this he meant that we can construct, bow down and worship anything we take pleasure in. And we can take pleasure in anything. Indeed, God has given us the capacity to delight in whatever we want. We can delight in people, in places, in material possessions, in our vocation and in our reputation. We can also take pleasure in our rules. You see, the human heart is also a factory of rules, and therefore a factory of legalism. I pray that what you have just read will help you look into your own heart, and that by the grace of God, it will enable you to evaluate the degree to which the rules you are living by, are indeed God's rules.

---

43 Are You Legalistic? Legalism, Grace, and the Motivation for Obedience, By Dr. Robert G. Spinney (http://www.hartsvillereformedbaptist.com/roblegal.htm)

44 Edward T. Welch, "Is Biblical-Nouthetic Counseling Legalistic? Reexamination of a Biblical Theme," *The Journal of Pastoral Practice* 11, no. 1 (1992): 13.